I0408134

Dolphin Coloring Book For Adults

Dolphins Coloring Book containing 40 Dolphin designs filled with intricate and stress relieving patterns.

Coloring Books For Adults: Vol 14

by The Coloring Book People

ISBN-13: 978-1542879590

ISBN-10: 1542879590

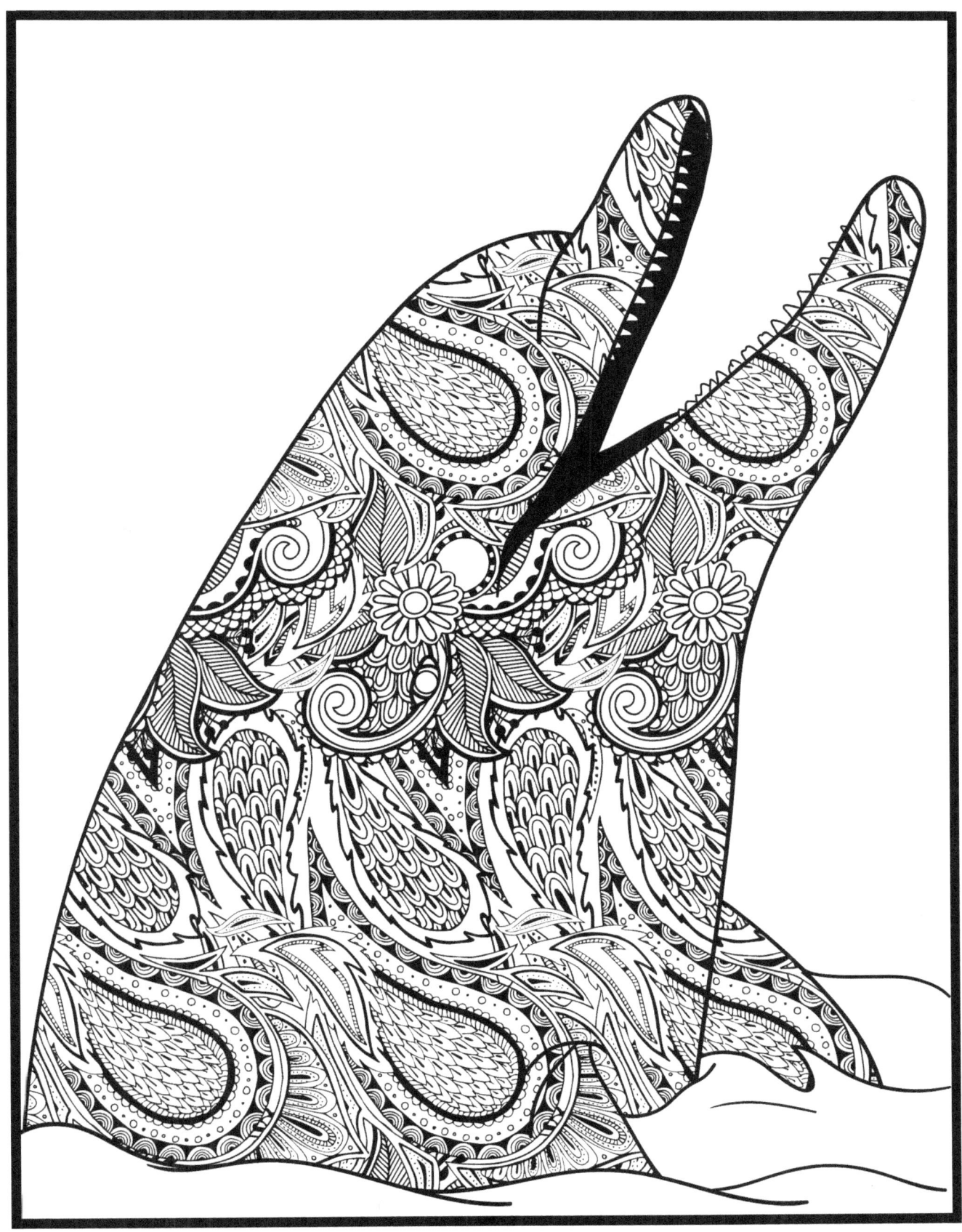

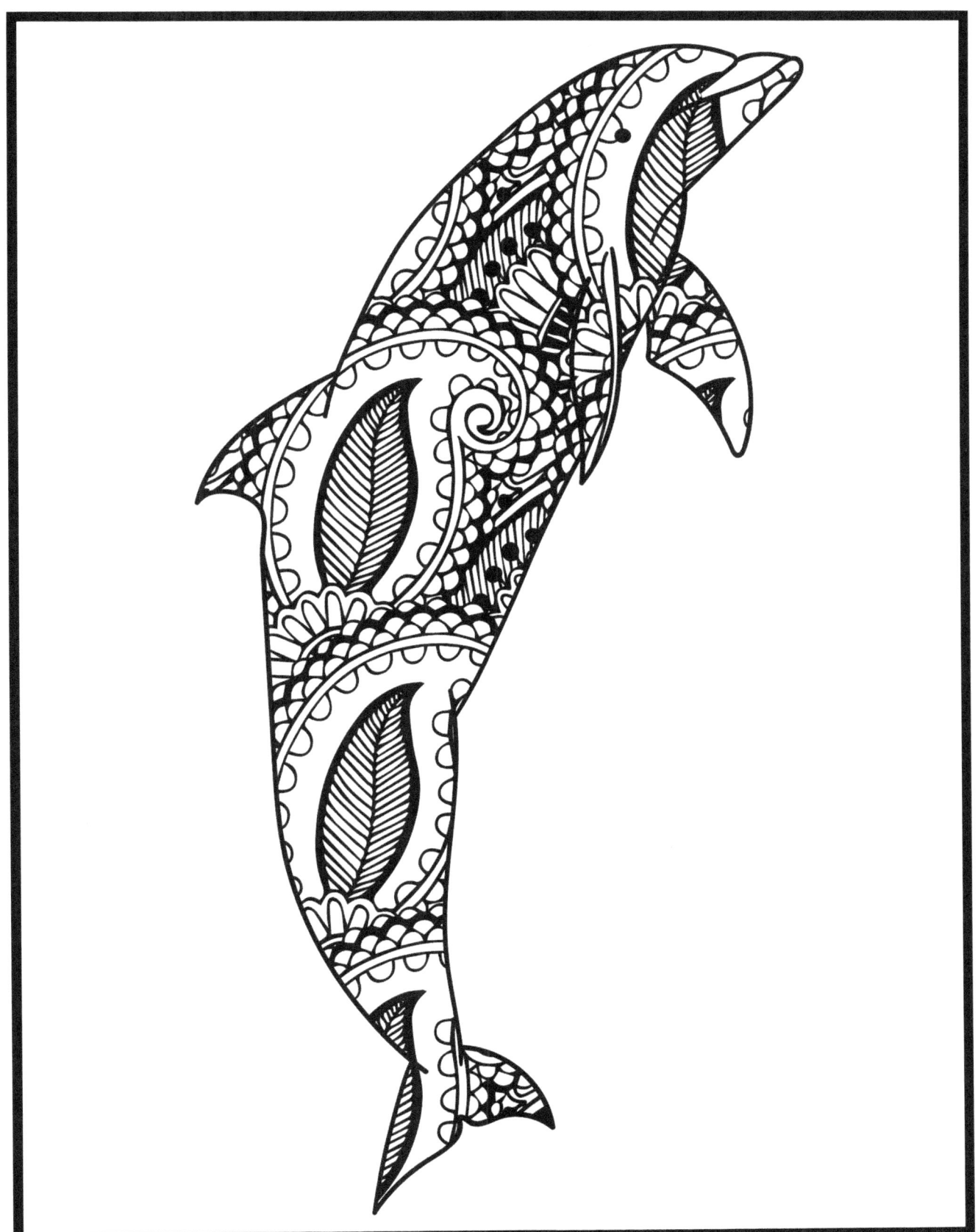

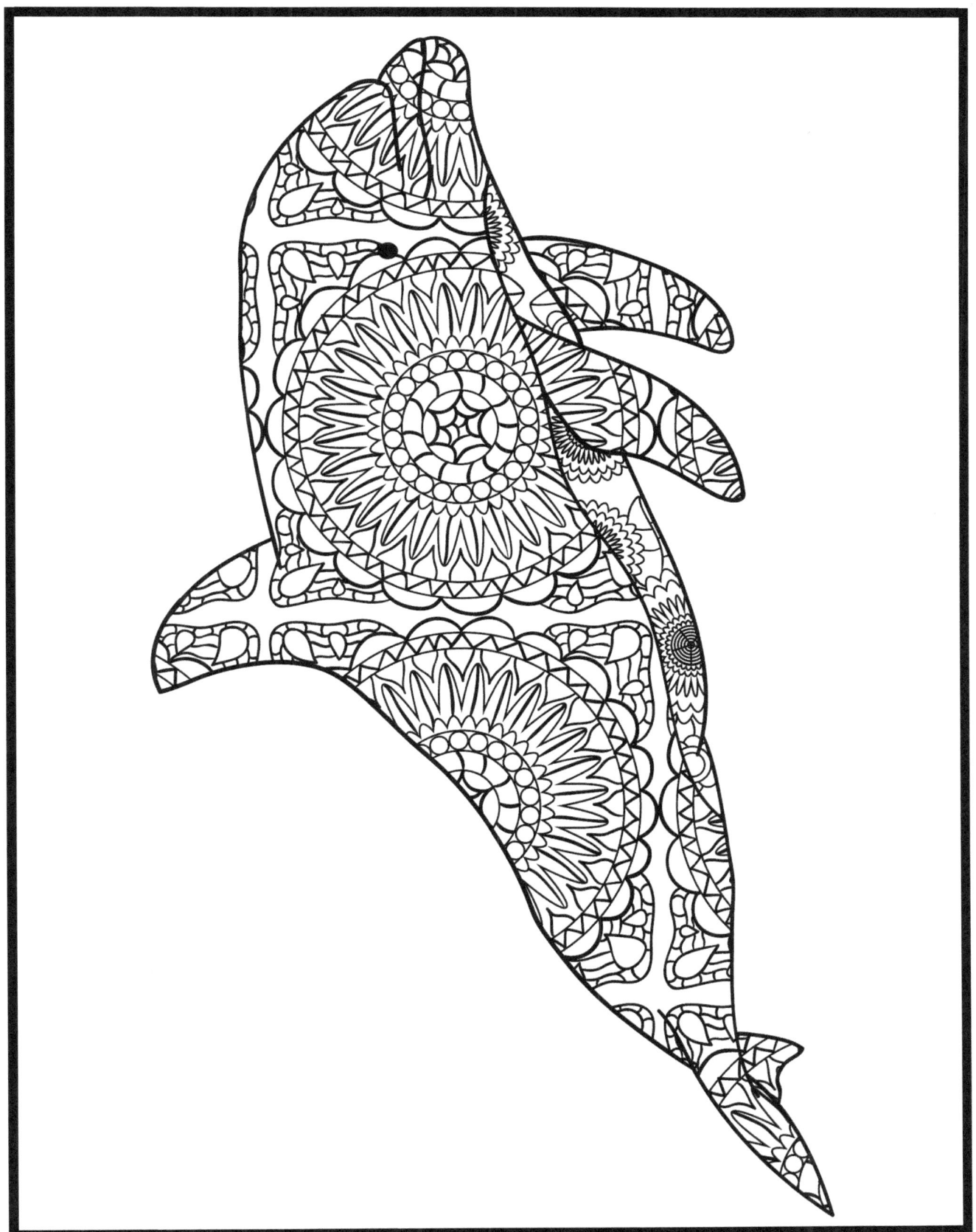

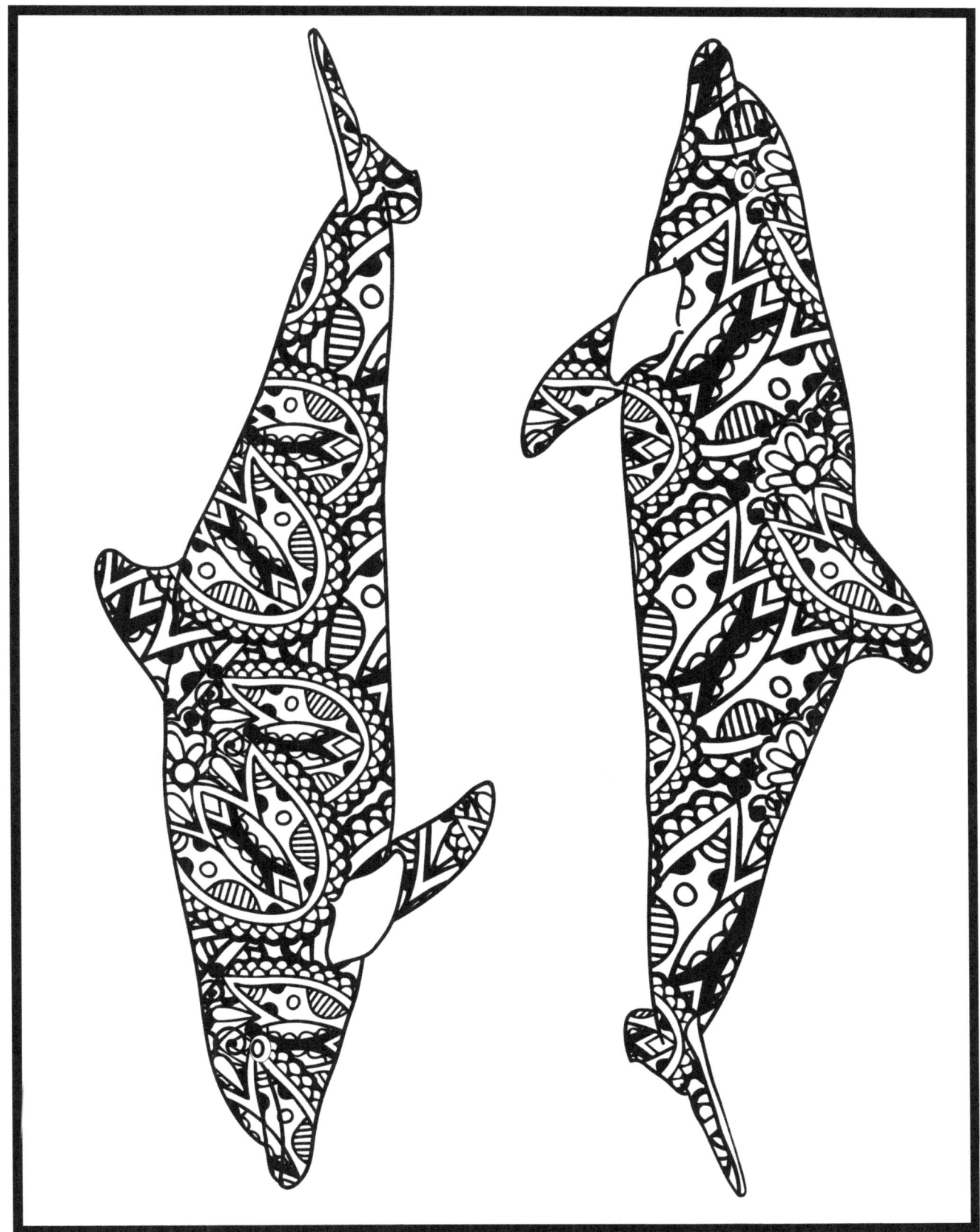

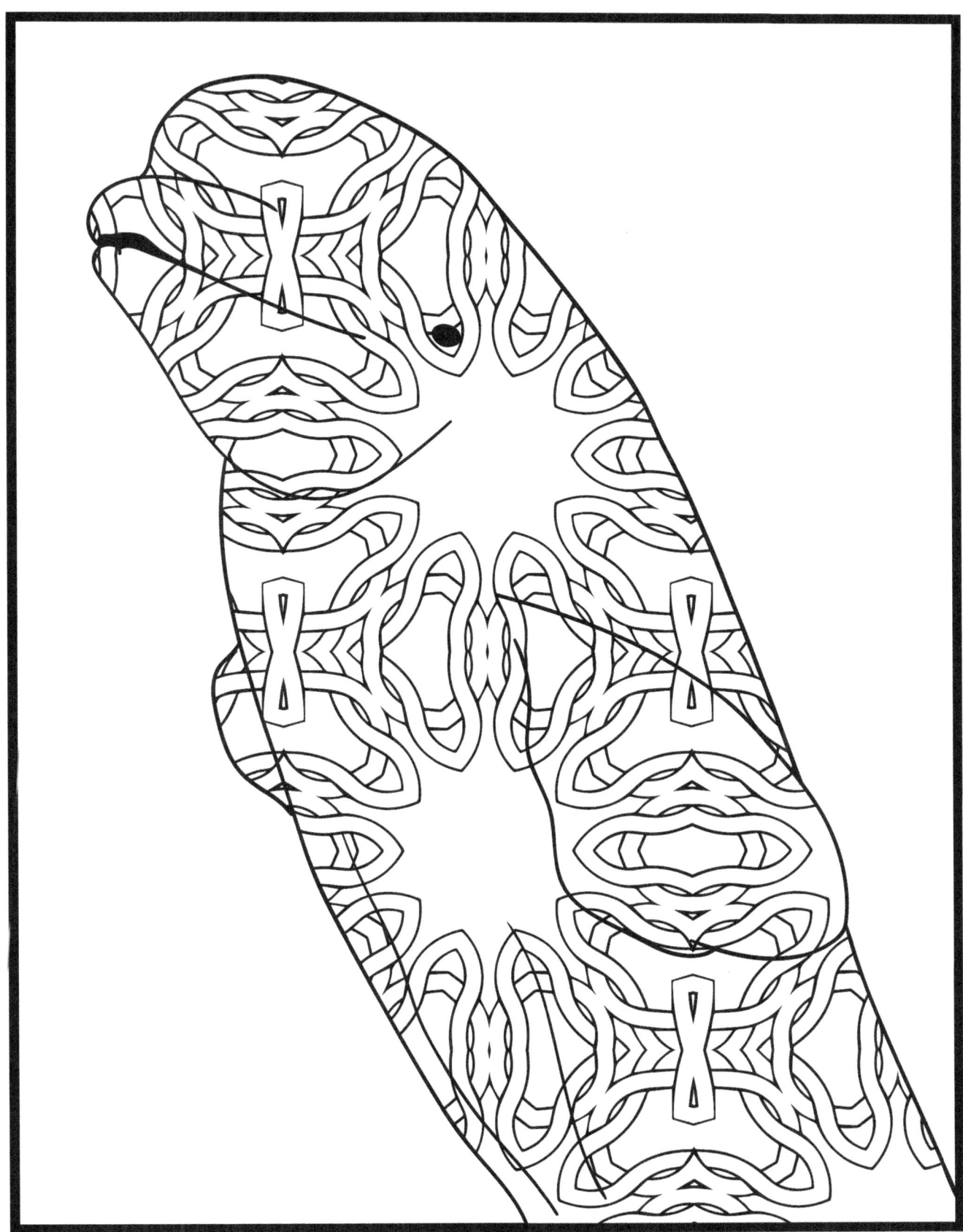

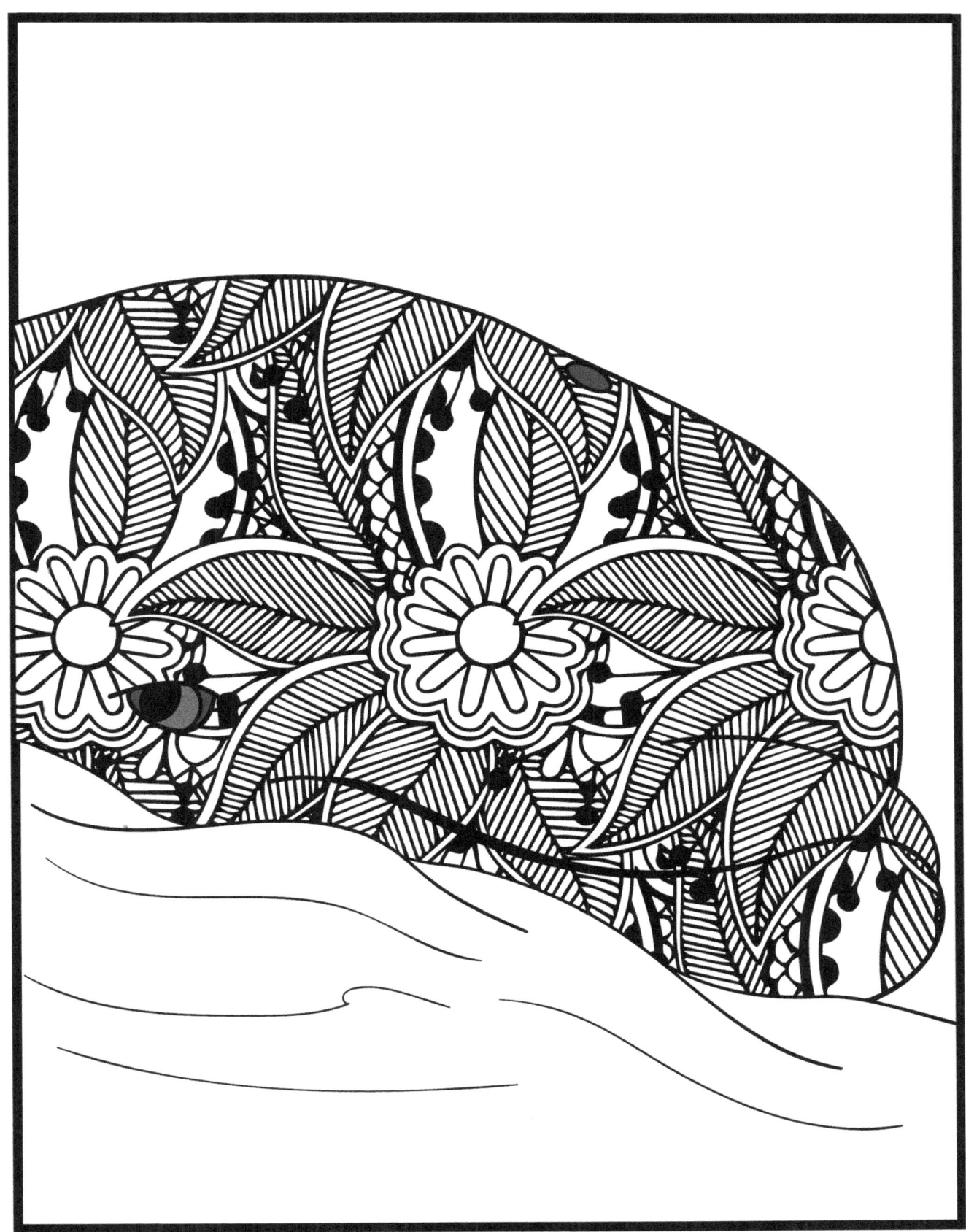

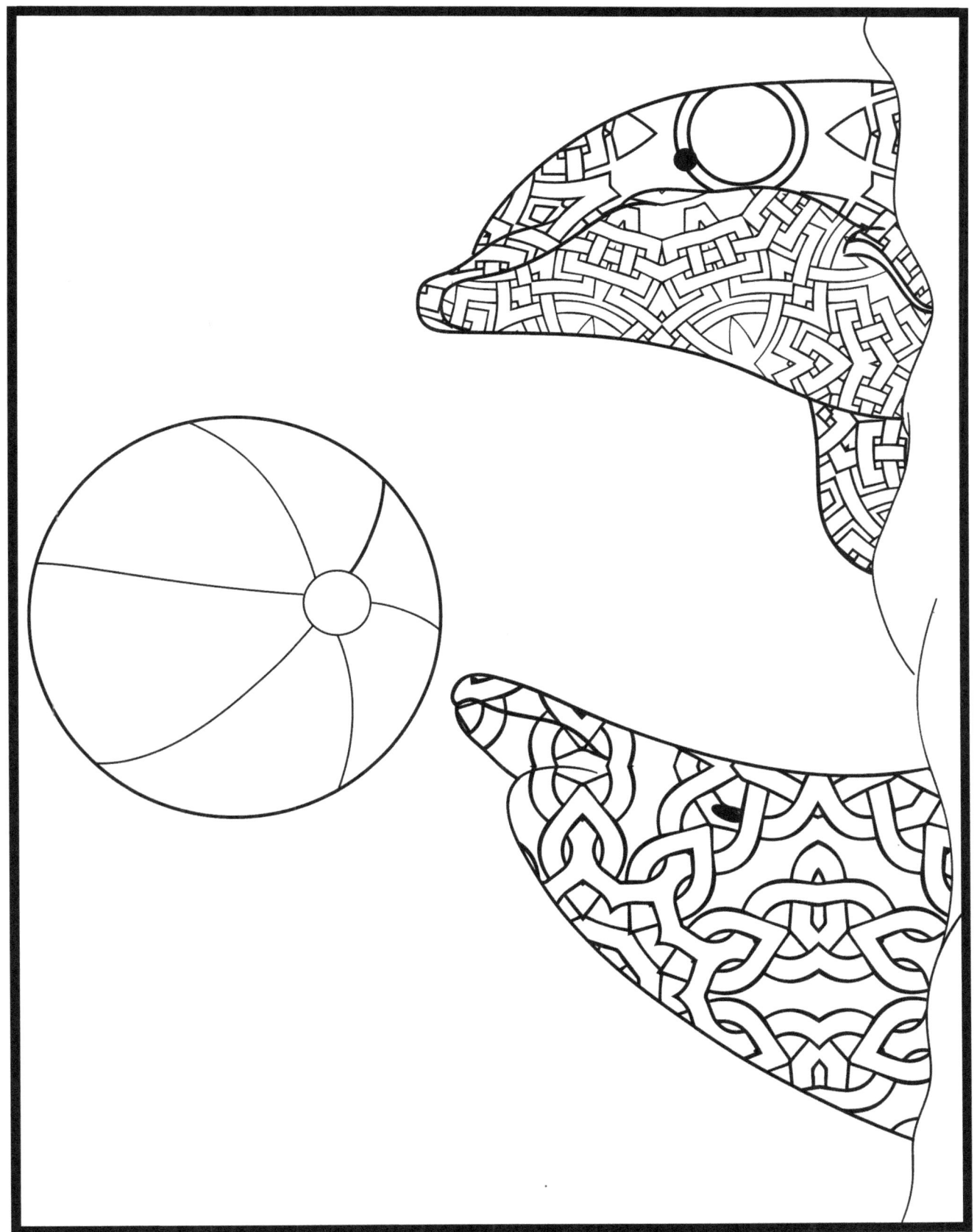

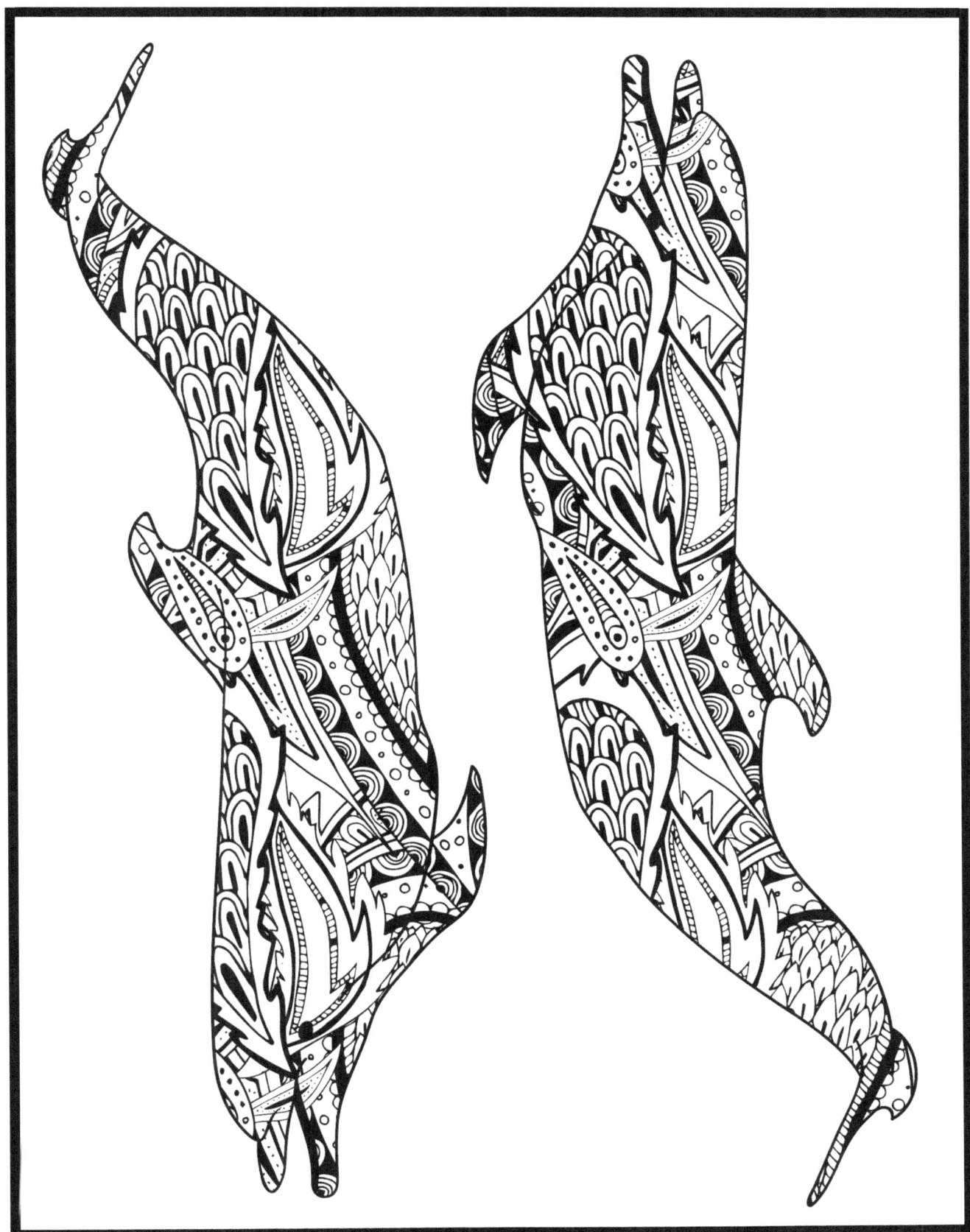

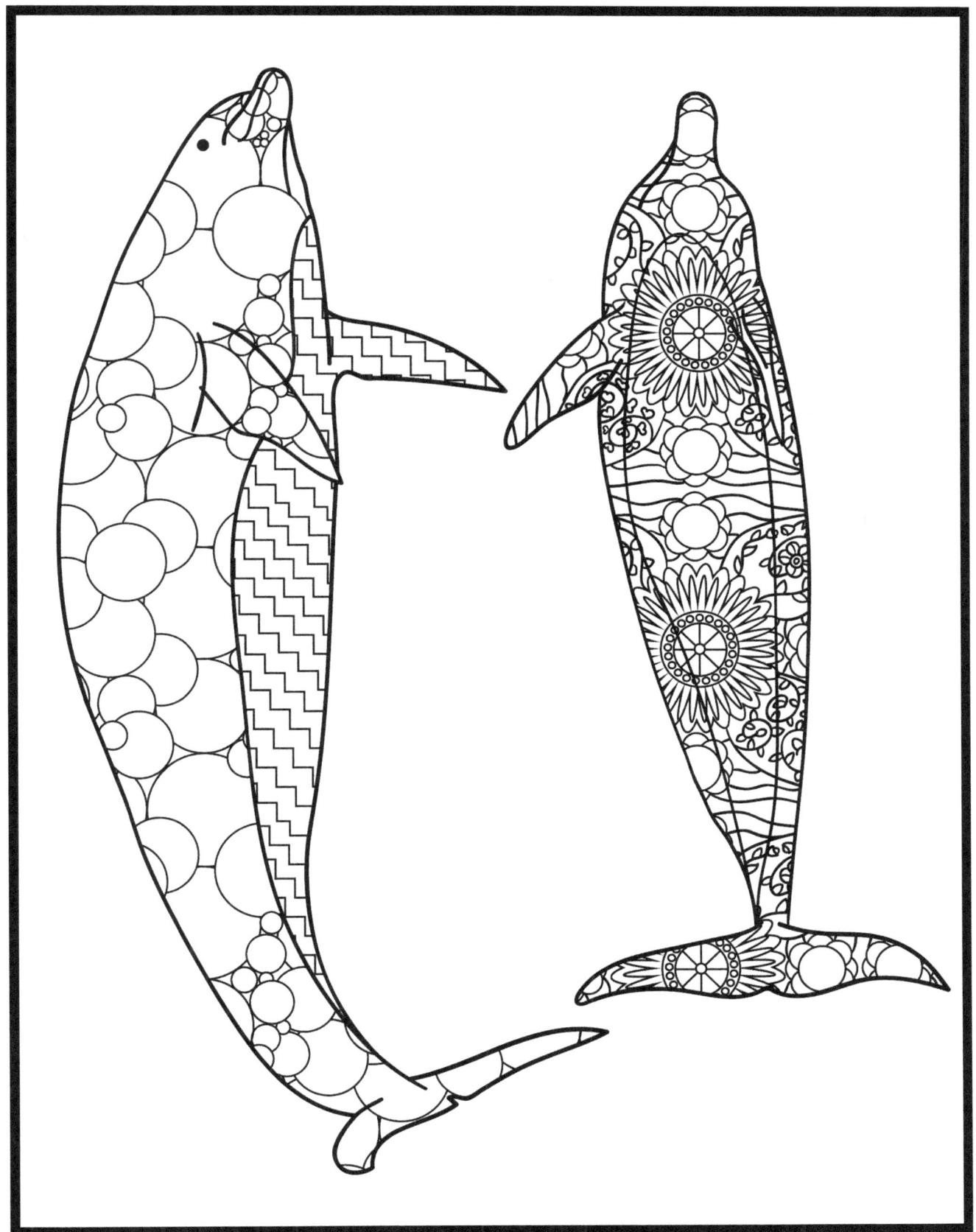

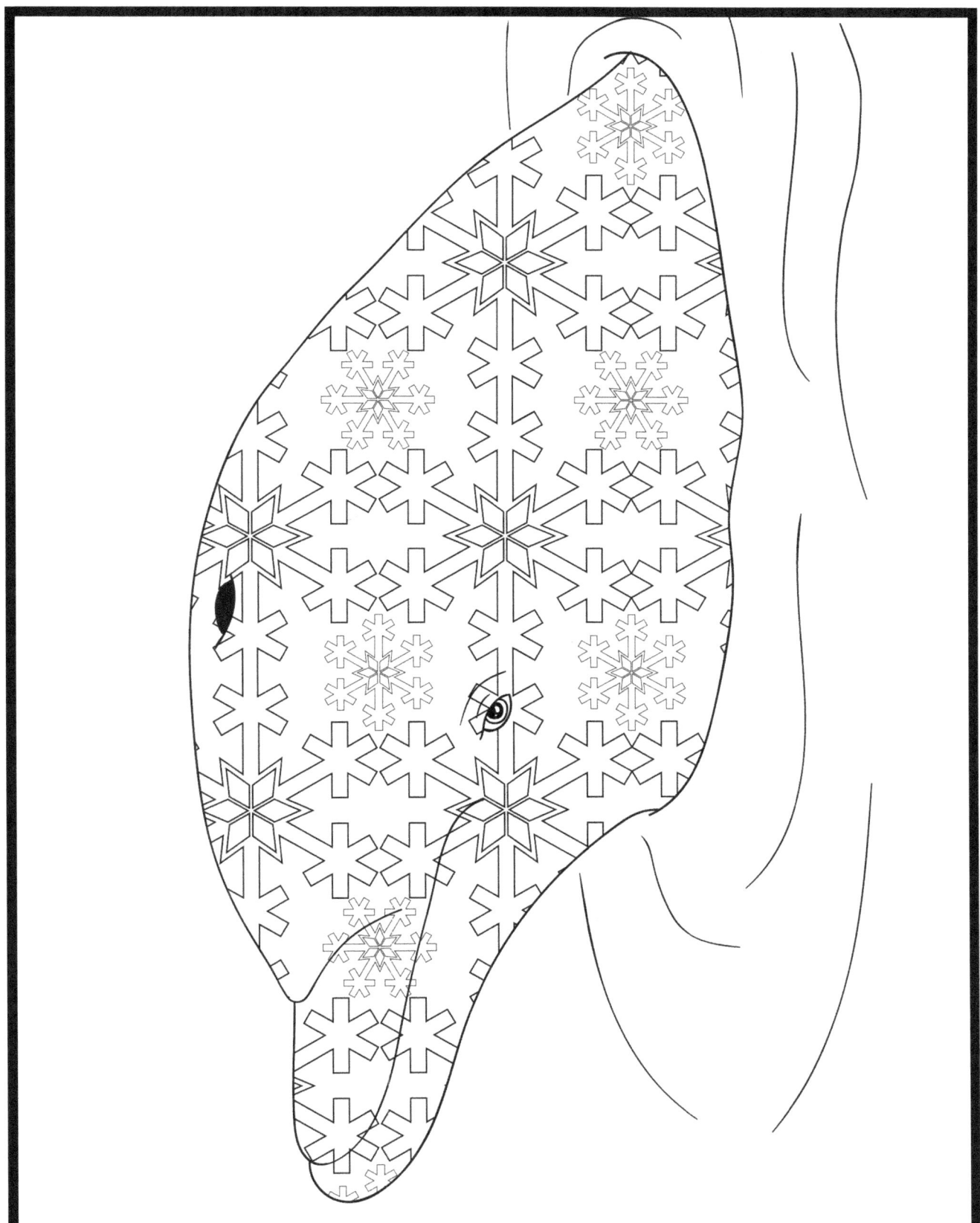

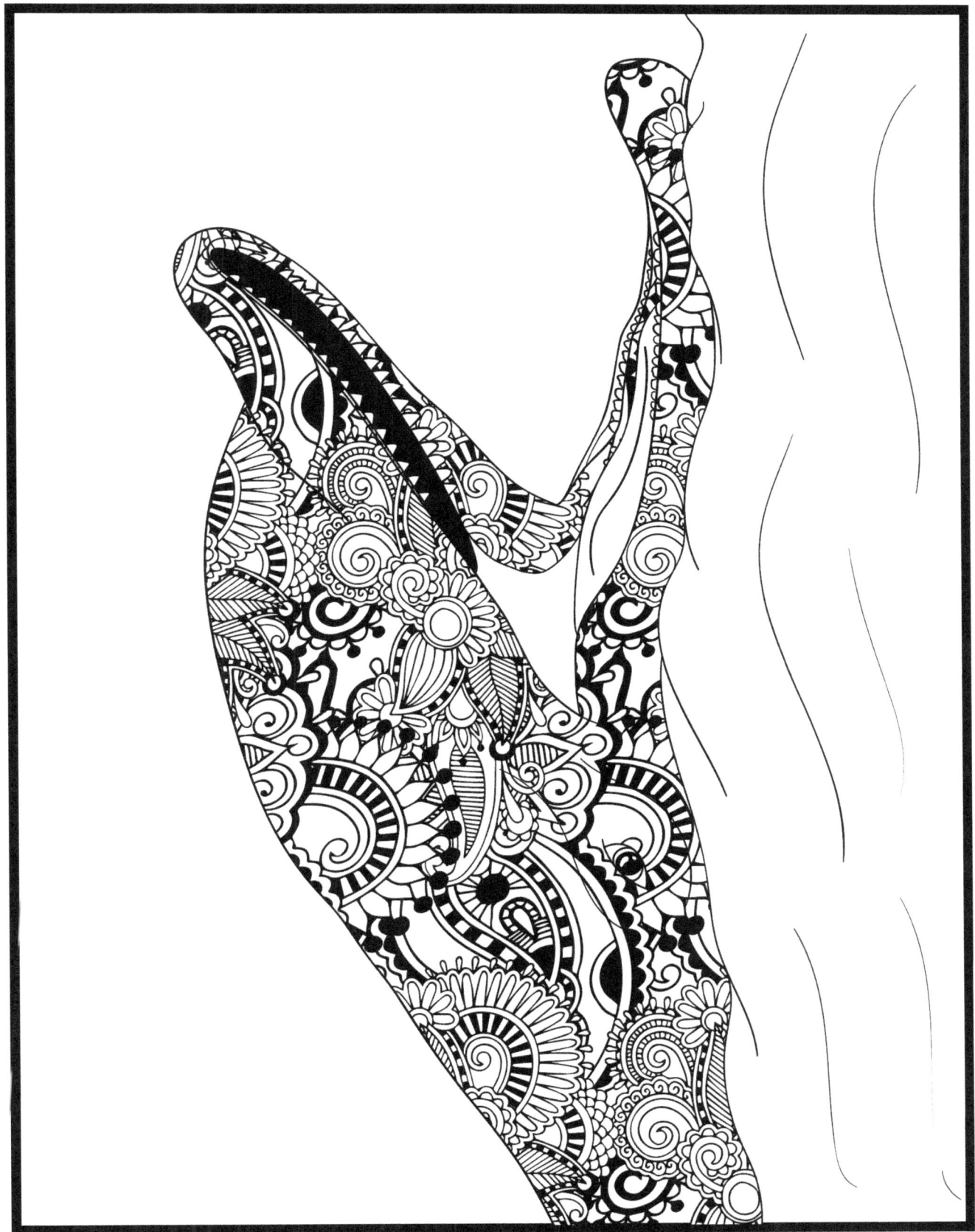

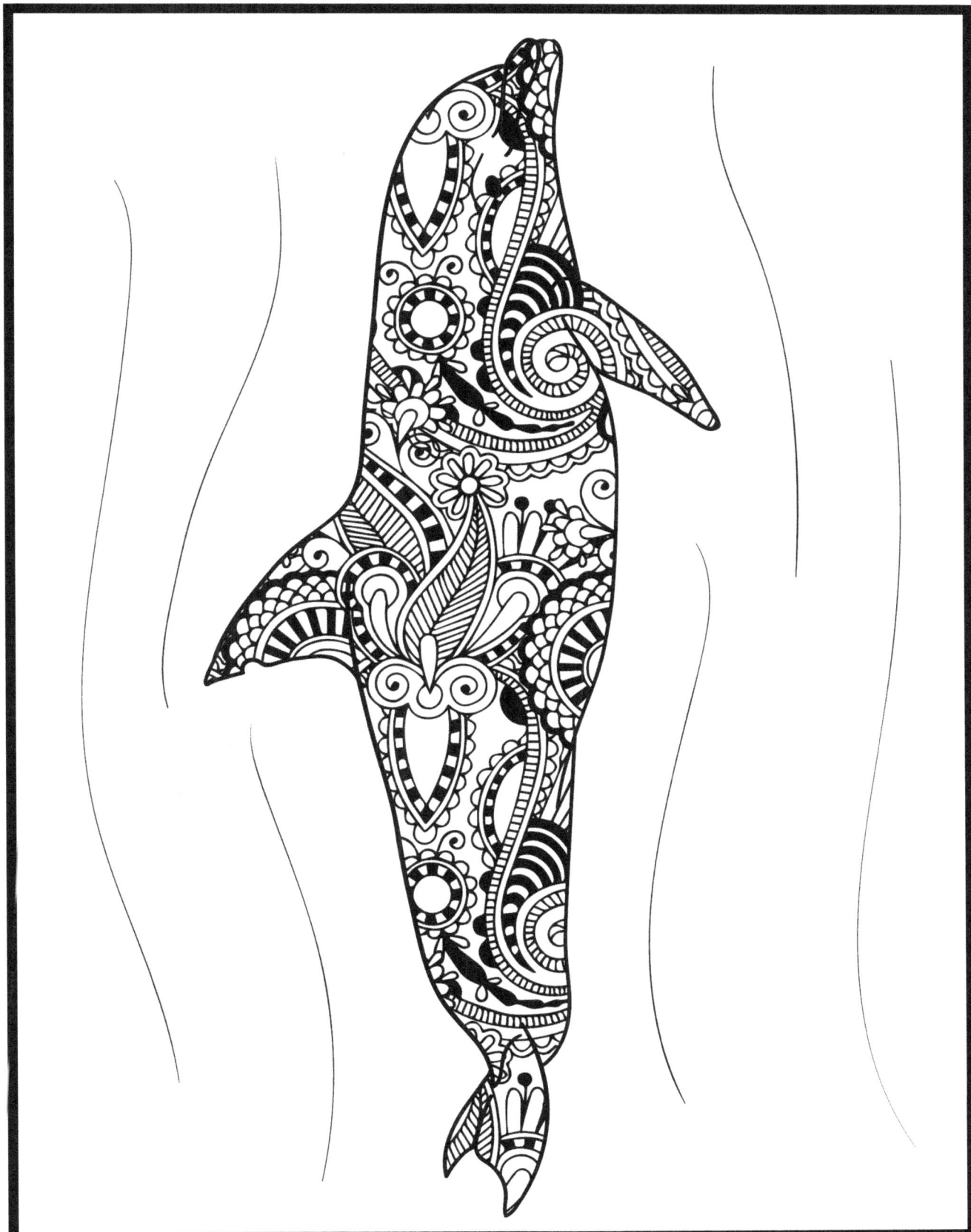

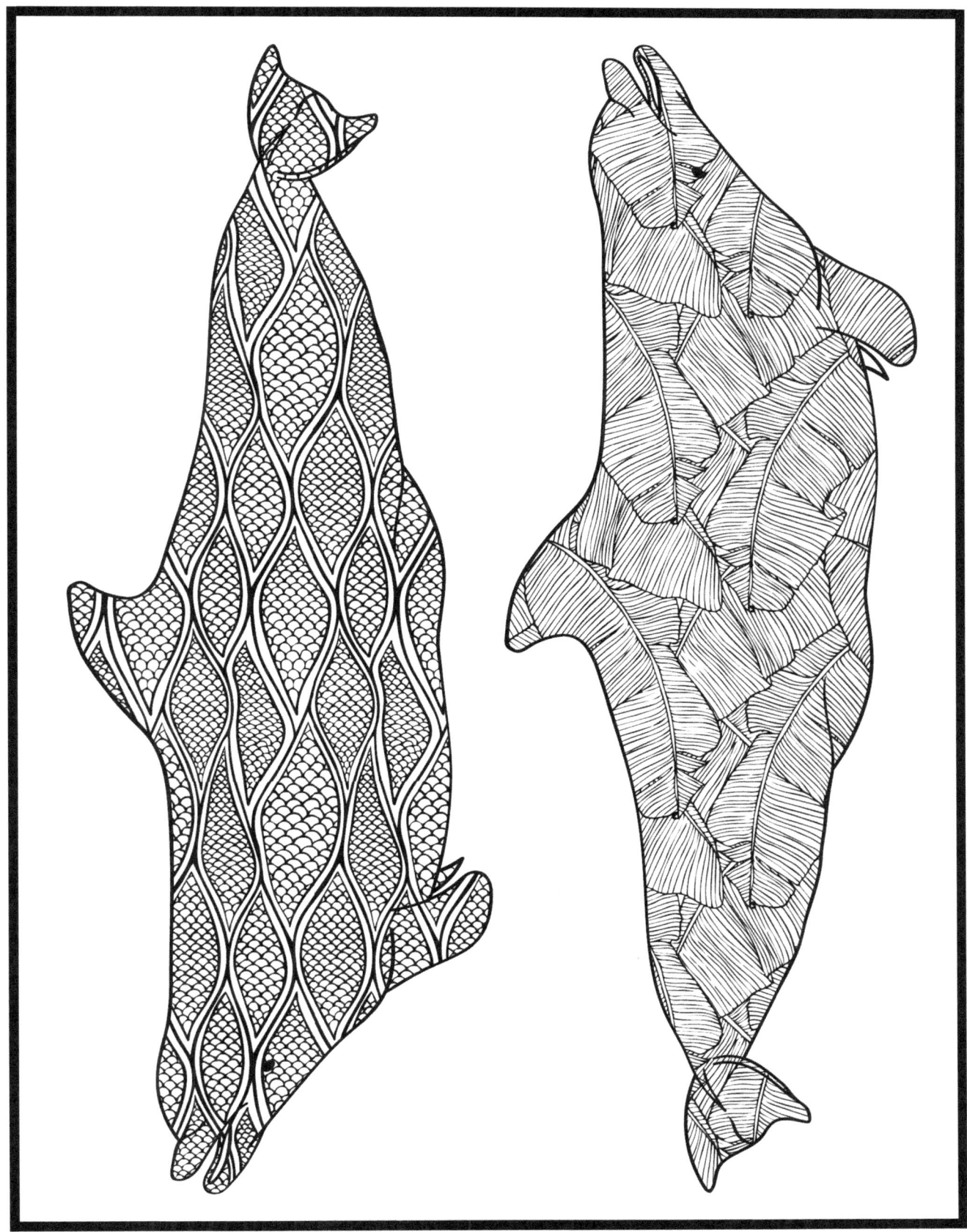

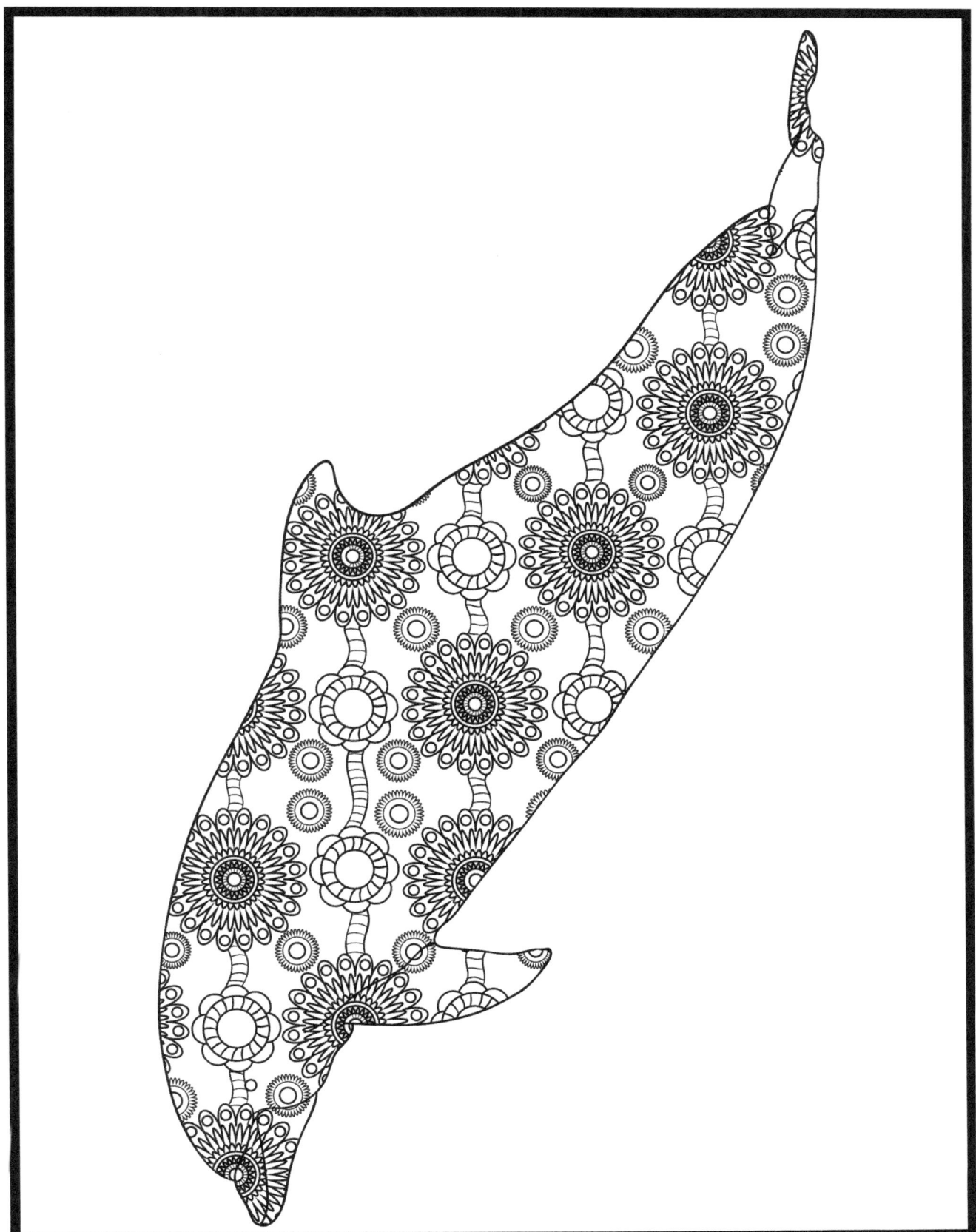

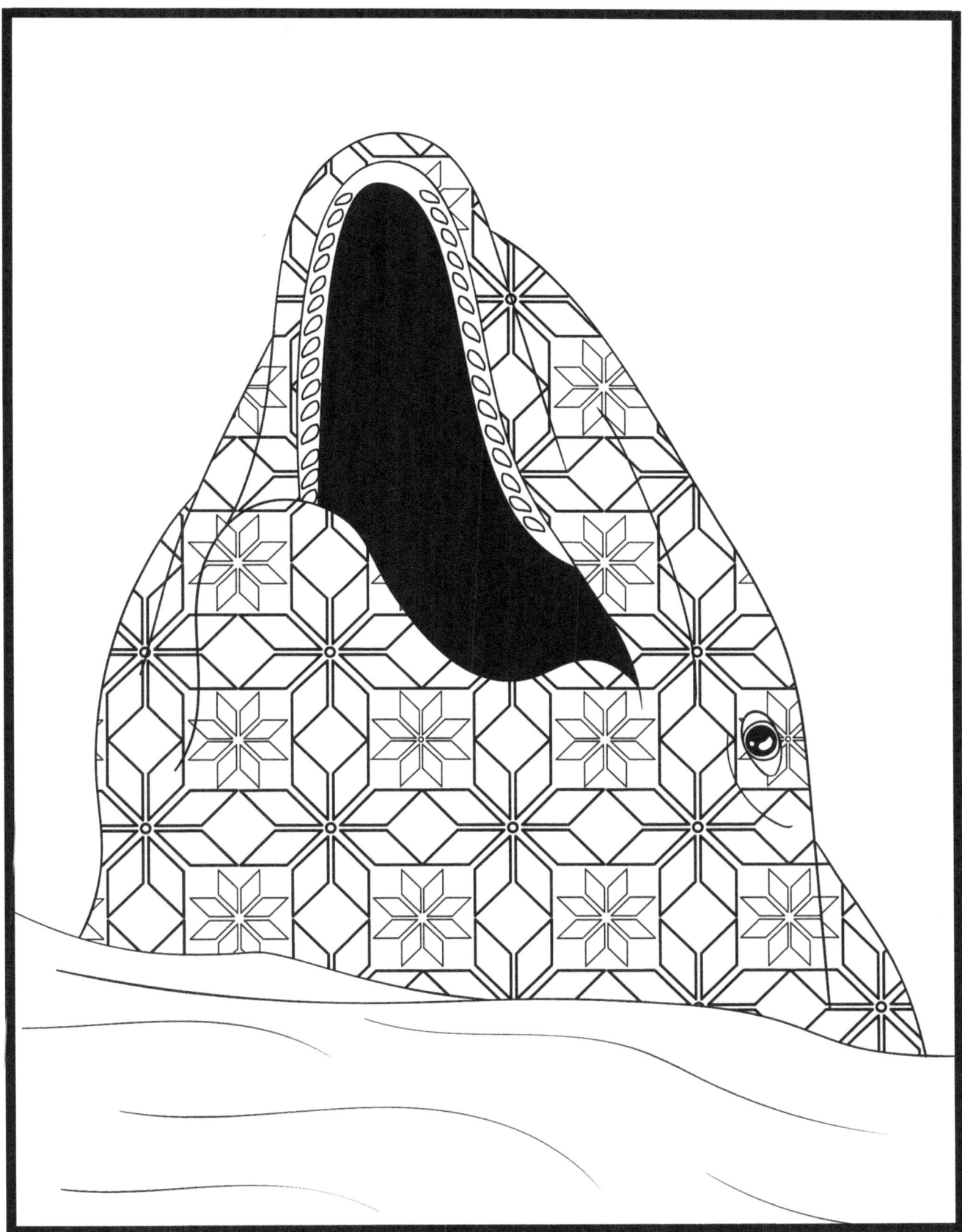

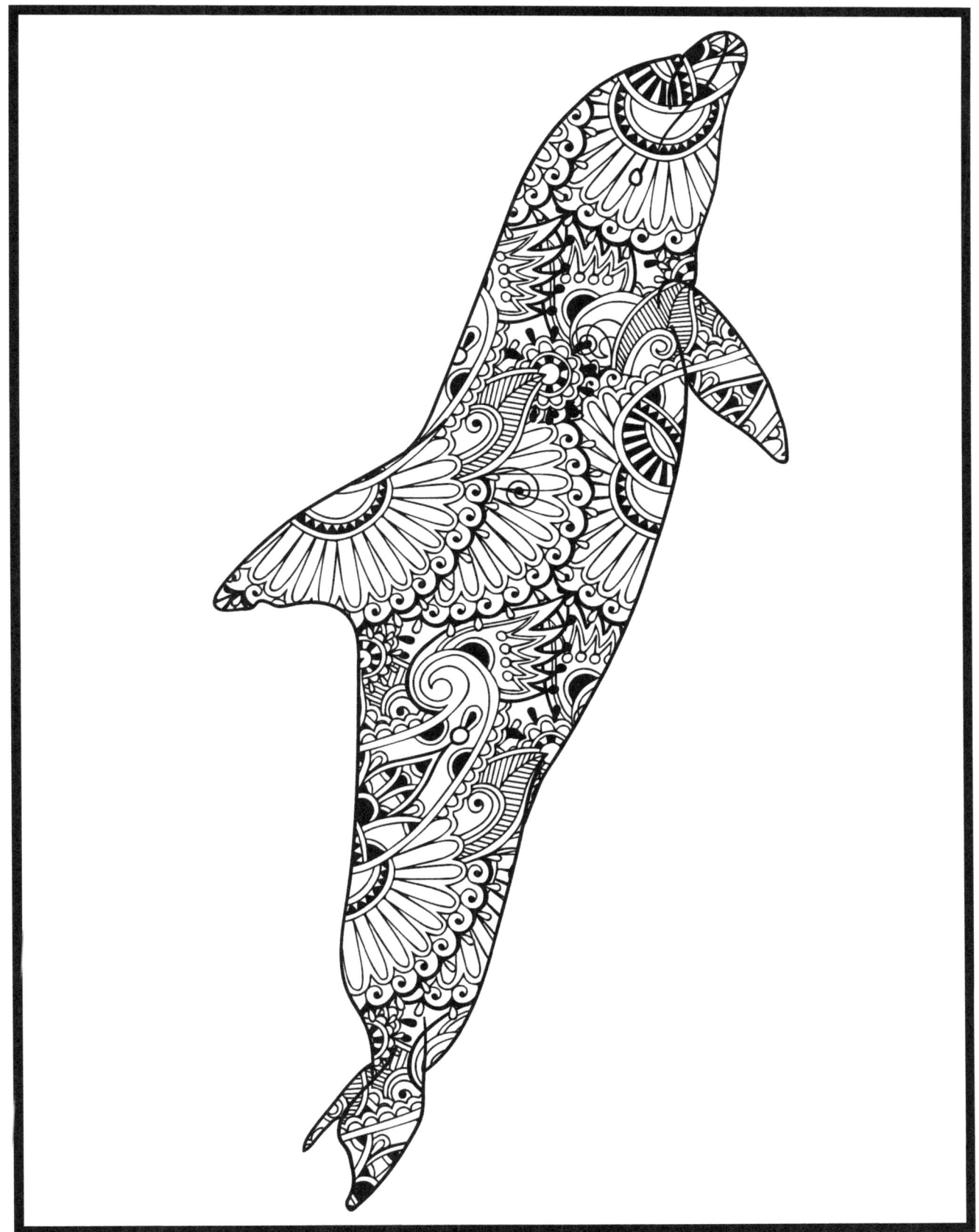

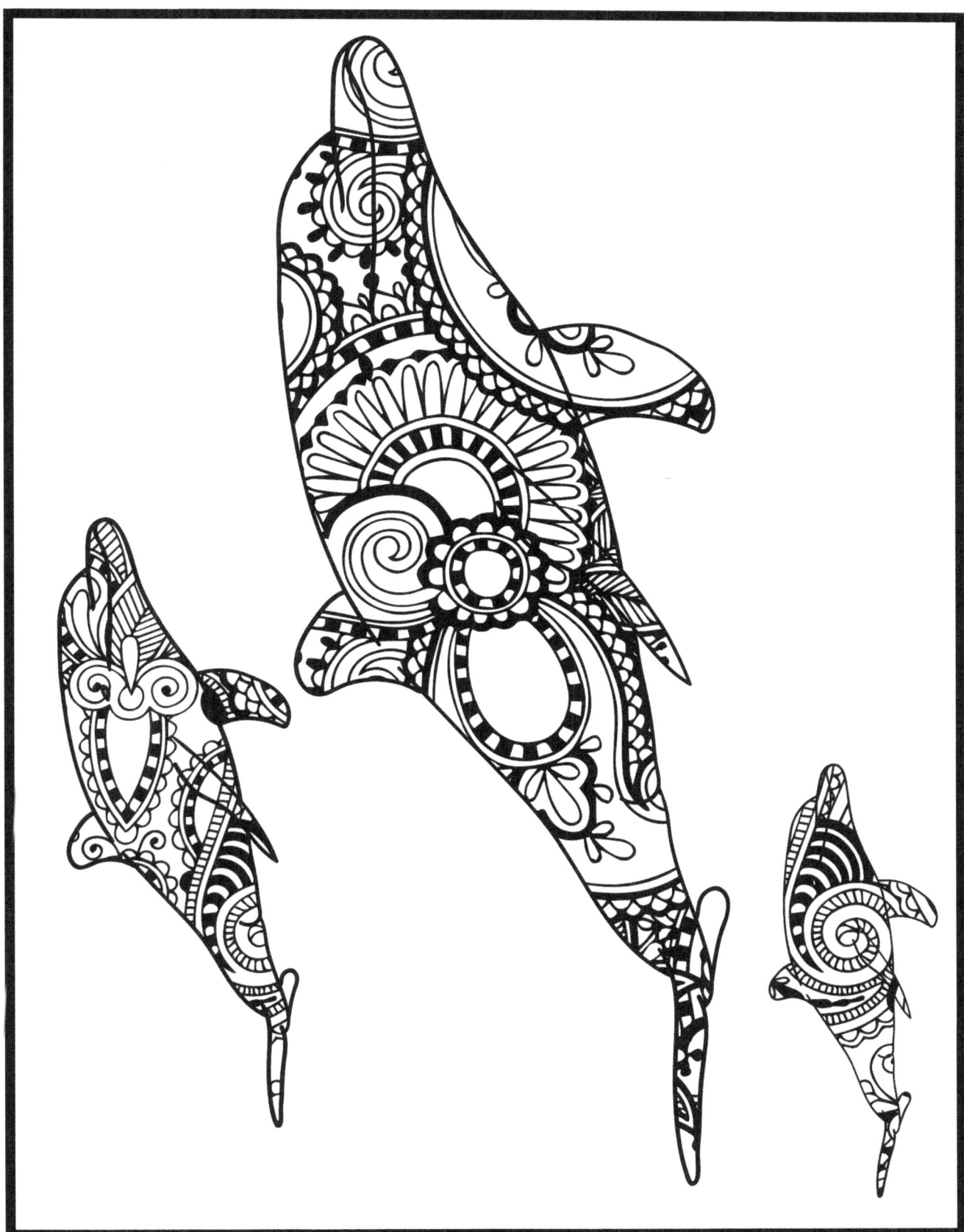

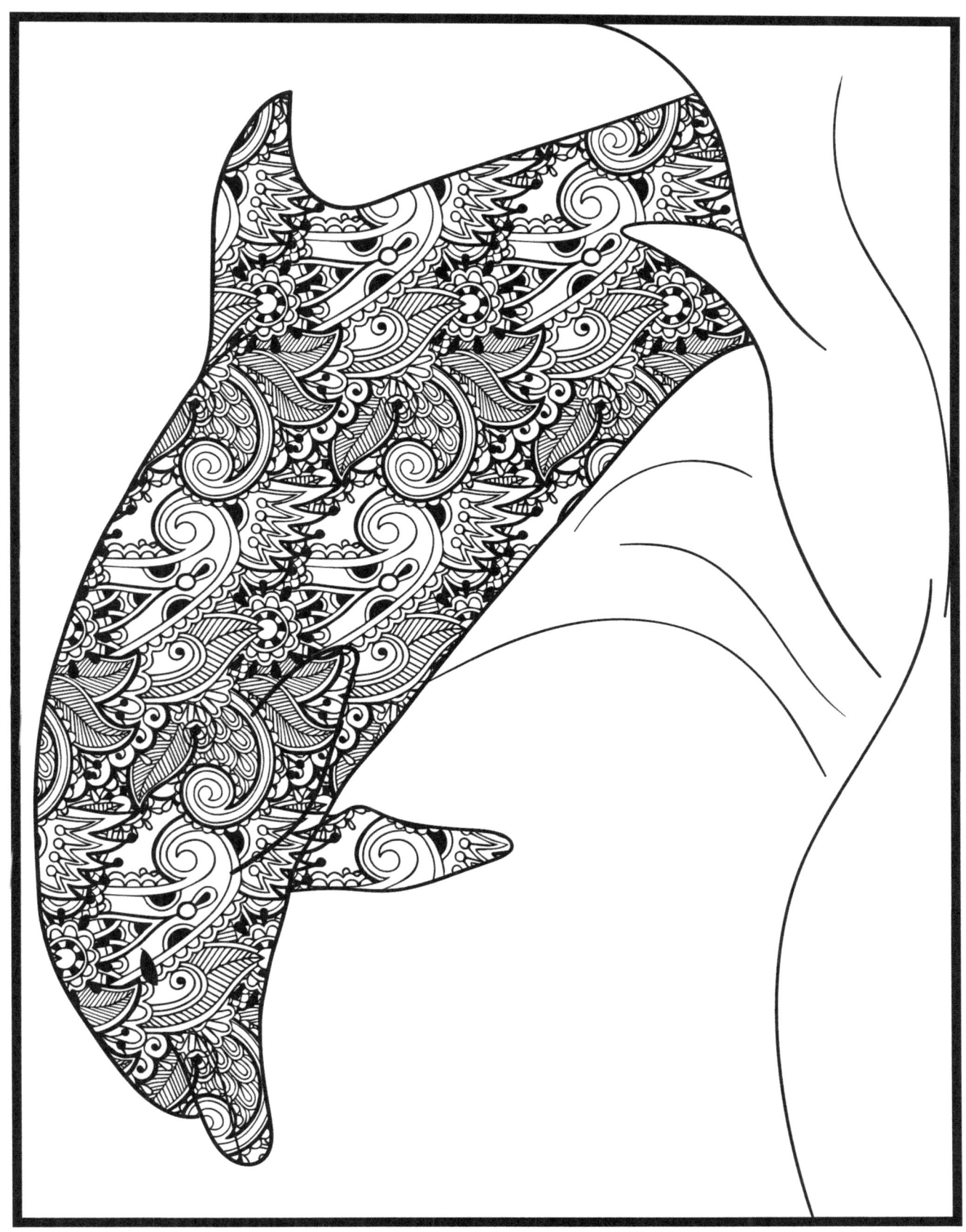

COLOR TEST PAGE

COLOR TEST PAGE